PANORAMA HAWAII

Scenic Views of the Hawaiian Islands

PANORAMA HAWAII

Scenic Views of the Hawaiian Islands

Photographs by Jack Rankin
Historical Photographs by Ray Jerome Baker
Written by Ronn Ronck

Mutual Publishing of Honolulu
Honolulu, Hawaii

Library of Congress Catalog Card Number 84-060785
ISBN 0-935180-10-9

First Printing November 1984
Second Printing March 1985

Produced by Bennett Hymer
Designed by The Art Directors, Honolulu, Hawaii
Typesetting by The Other Type and Typehouse Hawaii,
   Honolulu, Hawaii
Printed in Korea through Creative Graphics International, Inc.

The Wide World of Panorama Photography

As The Eye Sees It

The eye is a marvelous instrument. It sees everything. With a simple turn of the head an individual can survey the entire available landscape.

Cameras have trouble duplicating what the eye can see, as the eye sees it. A normal lens, the one that usually comes with a camera when you buy it, has an angle of view between 40 and 50 degrees. It takes a photograph that looks normal but actually can only capture part of the scene.

A regular wide-angle lens can extend coverage to over 100° but the wider the angle the more distorted the picture. Fish-eye lenses, with their extreme wide-angles, can sometimes pass 180 degrees but the resulting distortion is primarily useful for special effects.

The photographs in this book, taken by Jack Rankin in Hawaii, are quite spectacular. Distortion is practically invisible although it may take you awhile to get used to what you're really seeing. The Cyclo-Pan 70 camera, which took these unique panoramas and which Rankin helped to develop, is the culmination of a century-and-a-half of scientific thinking.

Like the human eye, the Cyclo-Pan 70 camera turns to "look" at the scene it is photographing. This turning motion is fast enough to stop most action and, because the lens can move in a complete circle, a single exposure can cover up to—and actually go beyond—360 degrees. It is even possible to capture the same scene on both ends of a photograph just as your eye would if you turned your head completely around.

The Cyclo-Pan 70 camera does not look particularly magical. It's well-designed but not particularly fancy, about eight inches high, wide, and deep. When loaded with a full 100 feet of 70mm film it tips the scales at 20 pounds. Interchangeable magazines allow the photographer to change film between exposures.

Standard Schneider Symmar or Super Takumar lenses (not wide-angles) are used on the camera, varying in focal length from 75mm to 210mm. Any of these lenses mounted on the Cyclo-Pan 70 will take a photograph ranging from 1° to 360°. Exposures are made with only the center of the lens, a fact that gives the negative a uniformity of sharpness from one edge to the other. This makes it easy for the photo lab to get a sharp print when enlargements are blown up to wall-size in height and to any length.

During shooting the camera is mounted on a regular tripod and the base is leveled using a built-in bubble. The lens of the camera can then be tilted up or down to photograph the desired scene. While the base remains stationary the top of the camera turns rapidly at just over a second for a full rotation. At the same time the film moves inside the camera and the picture is taken in one smooth continuous action from left to right. This operation is a delight to watch.

Focusing and f-stops are set exactly the same as on a regular, non-panoramic camera. Depth of field is also identical and the shutter speed settings go up to 1/1000th of a second. Most daytime photographs are taken at 1/125th at f16 using Vericolor film. The camera itself is powered by a pair of self-contained rechargeable batteries.

Contact prints from the 70mm film are 2 3/4 inches high with the length determined by the lens and degree of coverage desired. A 90 degree photograph taken with an 80mm lens, for example, will turn out 5.1" wide while a full 360 degree photograph taken with the same lens will be 20.4" wide. For comparison, a 90 degree photograph taken with a 210mm lens will be 13.1" wide and a full 360 degrees will be 52.5" wide.

A native Texan, Rankin got into panoramic photography through the back door. He was already a successful businessman in the mid-1960s when, looking for an investment opportunity, he and a friend, Ken Meeks, agreed to back an inventor working on a medical invention designed for hospitals. In return for the loan repayment and a percentage of the inventor's future royalties, Rankin and his friend put in their money.

The medical invention, however, never made it to the market and the two backers unexpectedly ended up with the rights to certain equipment which had been held in trust as security for the loan. The

inventor also turned over several hand-made camera prototypes. Rankin subsequently established a small California research and development corporation and for the next seven years worked on perfecting the rather crude prototypes.

In time the company developed a full system (cameras, projectors, enlargers, and printing equipment) for panoramic photography. Rankin's company spent over $700,000 to develop the Cyclo-Pan 70 system. Since only 10 cameras were manufactured before the company was dissolved in 1978 it is not hard to figure out that the development costs amounted to $70,000 per camera.

The value of the Cyclo-Pan 70 camera itself, coupled with its limited availability, have made it a true collector's item. Rankin's present company, Panorama Photography, has two of the cameras. One is now owned by Kodak and is on display at the company's George Eastman House in Rochester, N.Y. Another belongs to the University of California and is included in its museum of photography collection.

All of the other Cyclo-Pan 70s are in private hands. Each is treasured by its lucky owner, both as a unique tool for the working photographer and as a supreme example of contemporary camera-making art.

II

The Idea Takes Shape

Photographers have long sought to produce the kinds of panoramic views found in this book. In the pioneering days of photography the camera was simply pointed in a new direction after every exposure. This technique created a series of pictures with each new shot overlapping the last. With a well-planned succession of such overlaps the early photographers came up with primitive 360 degree views.

Louis Jacques Mande Daguerre (1789-1851), a Frenchman, and William Henry Fox Talbot (1800-1877), an Englishman, were the two founding fathers of photography. Daguerre, who discovered the so-called "latent image" in 1835, made his first "daguerreotype" two years later. His process produced one-of-a-kind pictures on copper plates coated with silver iodide.

Talbot used the word "calotype" to describe his photographs. He made the first negative in 1835 and developed a process to transfer this negative image onto pieces of paper. Numerous prints could be made from one exposure. These calotypes could be trimmed and mounted in whatever manner pleased the photographer.

It was Talbot who took the first known panoramic sequence of photographs in 1843 in Orleans, France. His book, *The Pencil of Nature* (1844), issued in six sections, was the first commercially published work to be illustrated with photographic prints. In 1846 he made his best-known panorama, a set of two views taken of his photographic factory in Reading, England.

The earliest surviving panoramic sequence taken in Hawaii was shot by Charles Leander Weed (1824-1903), a photographer who came to Honolulu in March 1865 from San Francisco. He was already a well-known California photographer before his arrival, having earned his reputation with a series of large landscape views that he'd taken the year before during an expedition through Yosemite Valley. These photographs, made from 17" × 22" glass-plate negatives were displayed prominently in the San Francisco gallery of Lawrence and Houseworth.

Leaving the gallery to manage his work in California, Weed sailed to Hawaii along with a brother and sister. Here they visited a third brother, Frederick M. Weed, who was then living in Honolulu. Shortly afterwards the Weeds opened a photographic studio on Fort Street. During the summer Charles Weed completed a wide range of portraits, twin-image stereo views and landscape scenes.

One morning Weed set up his large wet plate camera on the rooftop of Oahu Prison. This brick-walled facility sat on a coral island, at the end of a causeway named Prison Road that ran across the tidal flats to meet South King Street. He first aimed his camera toward Nuuanu and made a slow-timed exposure. A second exposure was made toward Punchbowl and a third toward the harbor. The Bernice P. Bishop Museum in Honolulu has a set of the resulting prints; if placed side-by-side they form a dramatic panoramic view of the city.

In July the Weeds temporarily closed their studio and traveled to Maui. Charles Weed took photographs of several sugar plantations on the island and then decided to take a pack-horse trip to the top of

Haleakala. From the summit Charles Weed took another panoramic series of three large camera views, the first ever made showing the crater area. When they were later displayed in Honolulu the Haleakala prints prompted one newspaper to enthusiastically report in its pages that "The age of wonders and art has not passed away."

All of the Weeds except Frederick left Honolulu on Dec. 9, 1865, and sailed away to Hong Kong. Charles Weed, as far as is known, never returned to the islands. But during his nine-month residence he left behind a small but outstanding body of mid-19th century photographs of Hawaii.

Weed's method of making panoramic photographs in Hawaii required nothing in the way of special equipment. He simply moved the heavy camera and pointed the lens in the direction he wanted. There were, however, a limited number of cameras with rotating lenses available in Europe at the time.

Frederich von Martens, a German living in Paris, invented the first of these cameras in 1844. It was called the Megaskop and was used to make panoramic daguerreotypes. The pivoting lens covered about 150° and the image was created on a single curved plate.

Martens' nephew, Ludwig Schuller, took this idea further. He fashioned a version of his uncle's camera for wet-plate photography and made his negatives on a glass plate. In 1856 the Scioptric camera was introduced by Ross of New York. This used three separate glass plates to capture a 120 degreee view.

During the next half century a number of rotating lens cameras were introduced in individual or commercially produced models. In 1896 an American patent for a rotating-lens, panoramic roll-film camera was given to Peter N. Angsten and Charles H. Gesbeck. Their camera was subsequently manufactured by the Multiscope & Film Co. and the first model was released in 1898 under the trade name of Al Vista. This was the first panoramic camera to be sold widely over the counter. It could take an almost full 180 degree negative using a rotating lens and five-inch wide roll film which ran on a curved guide in the rear of the box-shaped camera.

Kodak introduced its Panoram Kodak camera in 1899. This hand-held snapshot camera covered a 142 degree angle and could be used to take both horizontal and vertical photographs. The Panoram Kodak camera was sold in several different models by the company through the 1920s.

The Cirkut camera, introduced in 1904 and later manufactured by Kodak, was the most popular roll-film panoramic camera available during the first half of the 20th century. It rotated on a circular base by means of an adjustable spring-wound motor connected to a gear drive. A set of interchangeable gear wheels, stored in the body of the camera, enabled the photographer to control the angle of camera rotation and the length of film (up to 360 degrees) to be exposed. While the camera turned on its base the film moved at the same speed past the lens opening.

Five models of the Cirkut camera were eventually put into production, the last being discontinued in 1941. The Cirkut cameras are still used today, by photographers who take pictures of large groups of people. Its lens moves slowly enough for the photographer to start the picture and then run to join the group.

In the years following Charles Weed's sojourn in Honolulu, a number of photographers, both amateur and professional, experimented with panoramic sequences in Hawaii. But it was not until the turn of the century, when true panoramic cameras such as the Al Vista, Panoram and Cirkut became readily available that panoramic shooting became commonplace.

One particularly energetic photographer was Melvin Vaniman who took several panoramic photographs from a hot air balloon during a visit to the Islands in 1901. His photograph of downtown Honolulu, shot from above the harbor, was widely reproduced and distributed.

Photo by Edward Lair
Jack Rankin operates his Cyclo-Pan 70 camera which is suspended from an aluminum shaft beneath the helicopter.

Robert K. Bonine came to Honolulu about 1906 and subsequently established a photography studio on Union Street. He made portraits, landscapes, lantern slides and motion pictures. Bonine frequently used a Kodak 10-inch Cirkut camera in his work. Alonzo Gartley, a talented amateur photographer who was also general manager of Hawaiian Electric, used an Al Vista camera to take panorama photographs during the same period.

The leading photographer in Hawaii during the first half of the 20th century was Ray Jerome Baker. Baker (1880-1972) first visited Hawaii in 1908 from California and returned in 1910 to live here until his death at the age of 91. In 1915 the owner of the Honolulu Photo Supply, John T. Warren, gave Baker the negatives to some early views of Honolulu. Some had been taken by himself and others by Vaniman.

Baker, himself, delighted in the options offered by more than a dozen panoramic cameras. One of his favorites was a 7 by 17 Kodak model which he used to take over 300 photographs. About 800 of these large negatives still survive although they continue to deteriorate due to their fragile nitrate base.

Baker hung many of his favorite photographs on the walls of his studio at 1911 Kalakaua Avenue. His wife, Edith Baker, hand-tinted many of them and thus created some of the first "color" photography seen in the islands. In 1948 the photographer presented this collection of panoramic photographs to Emma D. Richey and her daughter, Gladys R. Van Dyke. Today these panoramas are incorporated into the larger Baker-Van Dyke Collection of still and motion pictures owned by Mrs. Gladys R. Van Dyke and her son, Robert E. Van Dyke. A number of

Baker's panoramic photographs (as well as two by Vaniman and one each by Warren and Richey) can be found in the present book.

Neither Jack Rankin or Ken Meeks were professional photographers when they first began developing what later became the Cyclo-Pan 70 camera. They knew little about the history of panoramic photography and had never seen a Kodak Cirkut camera. Every problem was solved as if nobody had ever solved it before.

Photo by Evan Mower
Jack Rankin sets up his Cyclo-Pan 70 camera in front of the Iao Needle on Maui.

After the development company was dissolved Rankin went on along, determined to make the camera pay for itself. He traveled around the country and improved on his technique while building up an impressive stock library of over 600 panoramic shots.

Some customers wanted Rankin to shoot for brochures and annual reports. Others were interested in single-piece murals. In 1981 the Hyatt Regency Kansas City Hotel commissioned Rankin to photograph a typical tall-grass prairie for a revolving restaurant on its 45th floor. The end result is a tourist attraction in itself: a majestic 186-foot seamless mural that's wrapped around the center core of the restaurant. Made from a single strip of 70mm film it is the largest known print of its type ever produced by the 3M Scanamural process.

Rankin and his wife, June, eventually formed a new company, Panorama Photography, which began operations out of their garage in Ontario, California. They soon were joined by another husband-wife team, Bill and Lois Lair. Bill is a building contractor who had first worked with Jack on framing the photographs. The joint talents and efforts of all four contribute to the finished product. Jack does the photography and laboratory work while Bill produces a wide variety of custom-made frames and builds the special printing and processing equipment needed in the darkroom. June mounts the pictures, puts them on frames, and handles the shipping. Lois runs the front office and does most of the administrative work.

Rankin first visited Hawaii in 1976 and has returned regularly on both commercial and personal assignments. The earliest photograph taken was of Diamond Head and Waikiki, a view that Rankin feels has come to symbolize Hawaii to the rest of the world. It is a photograph similar to his earliest one that appears on the front cover of this book.

When Rankin is out in the field with the Cyclo-Pan 70 he looks for a scene that is impossible to photograph with a regular camera, even one with a wide-angle lens. He does not attempt to create a mood in his photos and unless he has a specific target in mind the scenes lean toward the familiar or recognizable. Over the years he's discovered that viewers tend to appreciate panoramic photographs more if they have seen the landscape in person or are otherwise able to associate themselves with the image.

According to Rankin, the best time of day for shooting 360 degree photographs is at 12 noon. This minimizes the shadow patterns. As with a regular camera, Rankin keeps the sun at his back and normally uses a long lens shade to prevent vignetting at the top.

After selecting the scene he wants to photograph, Rankin decides upon a point of interest. Sometimes this is a natural landmark like Diamond Head or the Iao Needle on Maui. At other times it is a particular building, a body of water or even an interesting tree. Whatever the subject, it will be captured at the center of the negative as the camera revolves its full 360 degrees. This is not to suggest that every photograph Rankin takes is a 360 degree shot. Most of the time it is not. He is more interested in the scene itself than tricky shots and, besides, the perfect setting for a 360 degree photograph is difficult to find.

Rankin crops his exposures in the camera by choosing the lens that provides the exact vertical coverage required. Empty sky and useless foreground are eliminated so that he can achieve the maximum image size on each negative. Of all the techniques that Rankin has had to master with the Cyclo-Pan 70, he says the hardest has been the ability to keep the straight lines of reality, such as roadside curbs and fences, from appearing curved in the printed photograph.

Because he is a qualified pilot, Rankin finds great pleasure in taking aerial photographs from a helicopter. The remote-operated camera is attached to an aluminum shaft far enough down so that a 360 degree photograph can be taken without getting the aircraft in the picture. The lens is pointed slightly downward to avoid the direct glare of the sun.

The helicopter shots are taken without a gyro stabilizer. None is available that will fit, control the camera, and still be light enough for Rankin to handle. A reasonable stabilizing job is accomplished by stretch cords tied to the landing gear but helicopter motion, in the form of a curving horizon line, still shows up once in awhile in aerial photographs.

While the camera is suspended from the helicopter

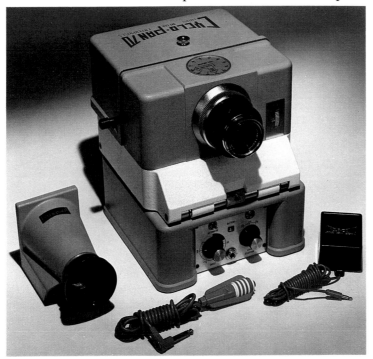

The Cyclo-Pan 70 Camera is approximately eight inches high, wide, and deep. It weighs about 20 pounds when fully loaded with 100 feet of 70mm film.

it is impossible to change lenses or film. It is therefore important for Rankin to load a full 100-feet of film before takeoff. For each shot he allows the lens to make double revolution and the final count averages about 50 photographs per roll of film. The final cropping is done in the photo lab, a luxury that gives the photographer total flexibility. Although Rankin usually uses a 105mm lens for aerial photography he recently switched to a 200mm to take a remarkable series of views above Haleakala that Charles Weed couldn't even have imagined a century ago.

Rankin say his next challenge is to develop a clear, tightly sealed housing so that he can take the camera underwater. He is also experimenting with high speed films to allow for photographing closer to the actual sunset and in other low light situations.

The future, of course, will always be ready to dazzle us. In the meantime there are the remarkable photographs in this book for us to look at and enjoy. They combine the creativity of a fine photographer and an amazing camera that provides state-of-the-art panoramas. Here is beautiful Hawaii, photographed by Jack Rankin, as the eye sees it.

Ronn Ronck

*A*bove Waikiki

> The Hilton Hawaiian Village beach and adjoining lagoon (center) in Waikiki were created for the hotel when it opened in 1955. Three years later the area was officially named Kahanamoku Beach and Lagoon to honor Duke Kahanamoku, Hawaii's 1912 Olympic-champion swimmer, surfer and canoe paddler. Only several hundred yards away once stood the home presented to Kahanamoku by the grateful people of Hawaii after his triumph at the Olympics. The hotel's catamaran pier juts out to the right while the Ala Wai Marina and Boat Harbor is to the left in the photograph. Farther left is Ala Moana Beach Park with its artificial Magic Island peninsula, completed in 1964 through the reclamation of approximately 30 acres of shallow reef bed.

On the Beach

< Sun and sand are the top attractions at Waikiki Beach, one of the most famous visitor destinations in the world. This photograph was taken near the heart of Waikiki, across Kalakaua Avenue from Hemmeter Center and the Hyatt Regency Hotel. At left, behind the coconut trees, is the Waikiki Beach Center. Some old-timers still call this area Tavern because of a succession of well-patronized drinking spots that operated here from 1917. The last of the line, the famed Waikiki Tavern, was torn down by the city in 1960. A beautiful park-like open area was created here for the first time since the mid-1890s.

From the Moana Pier

Photo by Ray Jerome Baker
Baker-Van Dyke Collection

∧ This 1908 panorama of early Waikiki is actually two overlapping photographs. At far left is the Seaside Hotel and next to it are a number of private bungalows. In the connecting center of the two photographs is the future site of the Uluniu Women's Swimming Club which was founded as an auxiliary to the Outrigger Canoe Club in 1909, a year after these photos were taken by Ray Jerome Baker. The Outrigger Canoe Club, itself, was founded the same year as this photo just to the right of center. Continuing to the right is the old Walter MacFarlane and Judd residences and nearly out of the picture is the Long Branch Bathing Pavilion. Beyond would be the Moana Hotel.

9

Queen's Surf

∧ At the turn of the century almost all of the beach across from Kapiolani Park was still under private ownership. Then, in 1908, the city bought the shoreline property parallel to the present-day park bandstand and began opening this patch of beach for public recreation. Chris Holmes, an heir to the Fleischmann yeast millions, bought a two-story mansion here from Charles Deering during the 1930s. During World War II it was used as a recreation center for servicemen and women. After Holmes died in 1944 the home was sold and, in 1946, converted into a restaurant and nightclub. The building and its famed Barefoot Bar was torn down in 1971 and all that now remains of the club is the floor of the main dining room (below the peak of Diamond Head) which has been covered and retained as an open-air beach pavilion. Today this clean stretch of sand, from the Kapahulu Avenue Pier to the War Memorial Natatorium and Sans Souci, is one of Honolulu's most popular seaside picnic areas.

Before the Moana

Photo by Emma D. Richey
Baker-Van Dyke Collection

Late in 1899 the Honolulu candy-maker, Gerhard Miller and Emma D. Richey, his sister-in-law, began taking panoramic pictures of the city with a small hand-held camera that produced pictures 3½ inches high by 11½ inches long. Richey took this photograph that year from the grounds of the Seaside Hotel, looking toward Diamond Head. At left is the future location of the Outrigger Canoe Club. Further along to the right was the Long Branch Bath Pavilion, the Walter MacFarlane residence and the Walter Peacock home which, along with the old residence of Queen Kapiolani, were replaced in 1901 by the Moana Hotel. The fondly-remembered pier, as can be seen here, was already in place before the Moana Hotel was built. The stately mansion just beyond belonged to the Ward-Hustace family. At the tip of Diamond Head is the new residence of J.B. Castle, later to become the Elks Club.

Old Waikiki Beach

Photo by Ray Jerome Baker
Baker-Van Dyke Collection

The Moana Hotel, the first modern resort hotel in Waikiki, opened in 1901. Its long pier and gazebo was a favorite haunt of strolling lovers. The old Outrigger Canoe Club buildings, at far left, were built between 1914 and 1916. Ray Jerome Baker took this photograph in 1923 from the Seaside Hotel looking past the Outrigger's beach pavilions and the Moana Hotel toward Diamond Head.

Feeding the Birds

> Not all panoramas need be dramatic aerials or unusual views of familiar landscapes. In this photograph a woman and her grandsons feed the pigeons at Honolulu Zoo.

< Diamond Head, the most famous natural landmark in Hawaii, was called Leahi or "place of fire" by the early Hawaiians. Fires were lit on the crater's rim at night to guide canoe travelers from the neighboring islands. In 1825 an exploring party of British sailors found calcite crystals on the slopes and mistook them for diamonds. They called the crater Diamond Head and the name stuck from then on.

$\mathcal{P}$ink Flamingos

> *Although symbolic of warm climates, flamingos are not native to Hawaii. These birds can be found at Honolulu Zoo in Kapiolani Park. The zoo started in 1914 as a small collection of birds and animals which were bought through public subscription.*

Kapiolani Park

V *Kapiolani Park was the first park in Hawaii which had extensive recreational facilities. It was dedicated in 1877 by King Kalakaua who named it after his queen, Kapiolani. Back in those days the park had both a horse racing track and a polo field.*

Today the sports are baseball, football, soccer, and tennis. Peeking over the trees at left is the Waikiki Shell where musical events are staged throughout the year.

*A*bove Diamond Head

∧ *In 1906 the U.S. Government bought 729 acres inside of Diamond Head from the public domain. For the next 44 years, until 1950, the crater was closed to the public and was occupied exclusively by the military. During World War II hundreds of soldiers lived in barracks which were constructed on the crater floor. In the late 1960s a number of rock music concerts were held here and the crater is now open for recreational use.*

Lovely Kahala

∨ The Kahala Hilton (center left) was opened in 1964. It is a favorite hotel for visiting celebrities and travelers who want to reside away from Waikiki. Behind the hotel is the Waialae Country Club and Golf Course, home of the annual Hawaiian Open. The course was originally established for use by guests of the Royal Hawaiian Hotel on the site of the old Isenberg Ranch known as "Waialae." Diamond Head is at the far left and Koko Head to the far right in the photograph.

Hanauma Bay

∧ Picture-perfect Hanauma Bay lies in the extinct breached crater of Koko Head. A number of Hollywood movies have been filmed here, including Elvis Presley's "Blue Hawaii" in 1961. Because of its status as a State Marine Conservation District, Hanauma Bay is also a popular diving and snorkeling location.

$\mathcal{W}$indward Sunrise

∧ Oahu's windward side, was once prime agricultural land for rice, sugar and pineapple. The population here has more than doubled since Hawaii became a state in 1959 and today it is one of the fastest growing areas in Hawaii. This photograph was taken from the Lanikai Bunkers area. The two Moku Lua islands area at left and the bay with the graceful curve in the distance at left is Waimanalo Bay. Makapuu Point and Manana (Rabbit Island) are at the far end of Waimanalo Bay. Beginning at the center of the photograph and moving right are the communities of Lanikai, Enchanted Lakes, and Kailua. Popoia Island (Flat Island) can be seen in Kailua Bay and behind it is Mokapu Peninsula which ends at the eroded hump of Ulupau crater. The fluted Koolau Mountain Range in the far background separates the windward side of Oahu from the leeward or Honolulu side.

23

*K*ailua Bay

∧ *Popoia Island in Kailua Bay is the center of attention in the above photograph. Mokapu Peninsula, home of the Kaneohe Marine Corps Air Station, curves out behind. The road close-up at right leads past the concrete marker into Lanikai.*

*L*anikai-Kailua

> *This aerial photograph (right) again shows the Moku Lua Islands, Makupuu Point at far left, Kailua in the foreground at center, Popoia Island in Kailua Bay and the Mokapu Peninsula. The panorama on pages 22 and 23 was taken from the peak of the hill that sweeps up just at the left of center.*

Lily Ponds

∧ Lily ponds have long decorated Hawaii's formal gardens but even most local residents have never seen these well-tended ponds. They can be found off the Nuuanu Pali Road near the water pumping station.

From the Pali

∨ *The view from the old Pali Road (reached by a trail leading down from the Pali Lookout) is one of the most spectacular in Hawaii. It was here in 1795 that the invading army of Kamehameha I from the Big Island drove the forces of Oahu to the edge of the 1,200-foot cliffs. Hundreds of enemy soldiers fell or jumped to their deaths on the rocks below. In 1845 the first horseback trail over the pali was opened by Kamehameha III who led a group of riders from Honolulu over the mountains to the windward side of the island.*

Over the Pali

*Photo by Ray Jerome Baker
Baker-Van Dyke Collection*

> *The Nuuanu Pali Road was widened to accommodate carriages and the first island automobiles in 1898. Ray Jerome Baker set up his camera along the road in 1908 and took this photograph (right) looking back toward Honolulu. Extensive planting and reforestation was being done at the time to stop the continual erosion of the area caused by wind and rain. The pointed mountain at top right in the picture is Lanihuli, a 2,775-foot peak that rises above the Lookout.*

$\mathcal{K}$aneohe Bay

∧ Kaneohe Bay has eight miles of coast, much of it artificially built through dredging and filling. Although it is a popular recreational area for sailing and fishing most swimmers head elsewhere. This is because there are no sandy beaches and the open shoreline is primarily silt and mud flats. At left is Heeia Fishpond, one of the few ancient fishponds still intact on Oahu. It was famed for its mullet. In the middle of the bay is Coconut Island and behind it the tip of Mokapu Peninsula which separates Kaneohe Bay from Kailua Bay. The Kaneohe Marine Corps Air Station airstrip is barely visible in this aerial photograph.

Old Kaneohe

Photo by Ray Jerome Baker
Baker-Van Dyke Collection

< Kaneohe had not yet started to blossom as a community when Ray Jerome Baker took this photograph in 1924. The area consisted of rich agricultural lands, full of bananas, pineapple, rice paddies and mullet fish ponds.

Haiku Gardens

∨ Haiku Gardens, near Kaneohe, was the private estate of Miss Wilhelmena Tenney, socialite daughter of E.D. Tenney, president of Castle & Cooke and the Matson Navigation Co. After her death in 1951 the five acre tropical garden became the setting for a charming country-style restaurant.

Ahuimanu Valley

∨ The peaceful Byodo-In Temple is the primary structure in Valley of the Temples memorial park in Ahuimanu Valley. Framed nicely by the Koolau Mountain Range it is a fairly exact replica of the famous 900-year old Byodo-In Temple of Equality in Uji, Japan, near Kyoto. The original temple is considered one of the most beautiful in Japan and is reproduced on the country's 10-yen coin.

Hawaiian Fishponds

Photo by Ray Jerome Baker
Baker-Van Dyke Collection

∧ These Hawaiian fishponds, photographed by Ray Jerome Baker in 1908, are located near Waiahole-Waikane Valley in windward Oahu. Faintly visible in the background is the region of Kualoa and Mokolii Island (Chinaman's Hat). The original black and white photograph, like some of the others in this book, was hand-colored by Baker's wife.

Byodo-In Temple

∧ Oahu's Byodo-In Temple, used as a Buddhist religious and cultural center, was dedicated in 1968. It took three years to build and cost an estimated $2.6 million. The temple and its related structures (a bell house, garden shelters and a ceremonial tea house) cover seven acres of the 45-acre Valley of the Temples.

Phoenix Hall

∧ *An integral part of the Byodo-In landscaping is the reflecting pool which compliments the temple's Phoenix Hall and its two wings. At left is the Bell House which contains a five-foot, seven-ton brass bell. It also has a twin in Japan.*

Sunset Beach

> Sunset Beach, the longest strip of wide sandy beach on Oahu, is also home to one of the world's most challenging surfing breaks. Modern surf riders discovered Sunset in the late 1940s and today it is the annual Winter site for several professional surfing contests. Sunset gets its name, naturally, from the fabulous sunsets seen from this area of the island.

< This photograph was taken from the road above Sunset Beach on the North Shore of Oahu. The housing tracts at Sunset Point (right) were opened for development in late 1919-1920 and most of the original homes were country retreats for residents of Honolulu.

North Shore

∧ Waimea Bay (center) is one of the magic names in surfing. This is where the biggest of the Winter waves, sometimes to 30 feet or more, explode over the reef and roll like freight trains into the shore. Behind the bay is lush Waimea Valley, once home for thousands of native Hawaiians. Today the 1800-acre valley is the site of beautiful Waimea Falls Park which contains an arboretum full of rare tropical plants, over 30 species of wild and domesticated birds, and a number of restored historical sites. Sunset Beach is around the coast at left. The road to the right leads to Haleiwa. At the far right is Kaena Point.

Sugar Cane

> Sugar was once Hawaii's major industry. The state's first plantation was established on Kauai in 1835 and exports were begun two years later. By the early 1900's the Hawaiian Islands had the highest yield per acre of sugar cane in the world. Sugar production in Hawaii has dropped in recent years but it is still a very important crop as evidenced by these extensive sugar cane fields on the North Shore of Oahu.

Waimea Falls

< Waimea Falls, at the interior end of Waimea Falls Park, drops 55 feet into the pool below. Four times a day champion divers leap from the cliffs in a demonstration for park visitors. Sugar cane fields cover the hills above the valley.

Haleiwa Hotel

Photo by Melvin Vaniman
Baker-Van Dyke Collection

< When the Haleiwa Hotel opened in 1899 it was one of Hawaii's earliest major show places and the first tourist destination hotel away from Honolulu. Its broad lawns sloped down to an estuary where outrigger canoes and other boats were paddled past to a nearby cove. A Japanese-style bridge (left) crossed the canal and joined a walkway to the hotel's circular lanai. Melvin Vaniman took this photograph in 1900. Ray Jerome Baker acquired the negative in 1915 and added it to his collection. In 1928 the hotel, which had originally cost $24,000 to build, became a private club and went through periodic renovations until old age and neglect led to its destruction in 1952.

Pineapple Fields

∧ Pineapple growing and canning became Hawaii's second major industry in the early 1900s. At first island sugar cane growers feared that pineapple production would take away their field workers and available land but neither happened. There were enough workers for everybody and land needs were different. Cane grows best in irrigated lowland areas or places where the rainfall is high. Pineapple can thrive in semi-arid areas with only moderate irrigation. These Dole Pineapple fields are found on the North Shore of Oahu. In the background is the Waianae Range. Mount Kaala (3,938 feet), the highest point in the photograph, is also the highest mountain on Oahu. To the left is the notch of Kolekole Pass.

Damon Estate

Photo by Ray Jerome Baker
Baker-Van Dyke Collection

∨ *Samuel M.Damon began developing his estate at Moanalua, Oahu, during the late 1880's. Ray Jerome Baker took this* *photograph at the Damon estate in 1908, looking from the later site of Fort Shafter, across the rice and taro fields towards Salt Lake.*

*T*oward Fort Shafter

Photo by Ray Jerome Baker
Baker-Van Dyke Collection

∧ *Looking from the later Salt Lake development site, Baker took this 1908 photograph across the Damon estate gardens of taro, rice and vegetables, and in the direction of what would later be the site of Fort Shafter. Farther beyond is Kalihi and Honolulu with Punchbowl and Diamond Head in the distance.*

Honolulu and Punchbowl

Photo by John T. Warren
Baker-Van Dyke Collection

∧ Honolulu was beginning to grow out of its small town boundaries in 1901 when this photograph was taken from the site of the new Pacific Heights development. Punchbowl, the ancient Hawaiian "Hill of Sacrifice" is in the background at center. The idea of using Punchbowl as a cemetery to serve Honolulu originated in the 1890s but it was not until 1948 that construction began on the present National Memorial Cemetery of the Pacific.

Arizona Memorial

V *The USS Arizona Memorial bridges the hull of the battleship USS Arizona which was sunk December 7, 1941 during the Japanese attack on Pearl Harbor. It now rests in 38 feet of water. The memorial, dedicated in 1962, is divided into three sections: a museum room, an assembly area, and a shrine room containing a marble wall engraved with the names of the 1,177 Navymen and Marines who lost their lives when the ship went down. Although the USS Arizona is no longer in commission, the American flag is mounted on its superstructure each morning and flown until sunset to honor all those who died in the Pearl Harbor attack.*

51

*H*onolulu

∧ *Honolulu, the capital and commercial center of Hawaii, has experienced almost a continual building boom since the Islands were granted statehood in 1959. In this panoramic shot portions* *of Waikiki are seen at the bottom of both ends of the photograph. In the far distance at left is downtown Honolulu while Diamond Head is at the far right.*

54

From a Balloon

Photo by Melvin Vaniman
Baker-Van Dyke Collection

< Melvin Vaniman, a photographer who visited the Islands in 1901, took this panorama of Honolulu from a hot-air balloon floating above the harbor. This photograph covers the area from Kalihi to Diamond Head. The first completely successful manned balloonflight in Hawaii took place in 1889. Joseph Lawrence Van Tassell rose from Kapiolani Park to an estimated height of one mile and then parachuted back down. Two weeks later he tried again from Punchbowl. This time, however, the wind carried the balloon off course. Van Tassell plunged into Keehi Lagoon and drowned. To the left in this photograph is Kalihi and Nuuanu Valley.

Aloha Tower

< Aloha Tower, at left near the docked passenger ship, was dedicated in 1926 and is 184 feet tall. At the time it was the tallest building in all of Hawaii. Today the Aloha Tower is almost lost in a view of the city's modern skyline but its bright spotlights can still be seen by ships as far as 19 miles away. Sand Island (center) is home for the largest Coast Guard Station in the Pacific.

Old Honolulu Harbor

Photo by Ray Jerome Baker
Baker-Van Dyke Collection

Honolulu Harbor in 1908. The channel entrance leads, left to right, to the Oceanic Steamship Co. Docks, the Inter-Island Docks, the Immigration Station, and the Healani and Myrtle Boat Houses.

Sailing Ships

Photo by Ray Jerome Baker
Baker-Van Dyke Collection

Ray Jerome Baker described Honolulu Harbor as "a forest of masts" when he photographed this dramatic scene in 1908. In another few decades these wooden sailing ships would vanish one by one as steamships took over oceanic shipping and passenger service.

Honolulu Skyline

∧ The modern cityscape of Honolulu is one of the most beautiful in the Pacific. Downtown and Punchbowl is to the left, Tantalus and Manoa Valley is at center and Waikiki is at right. The Ala Wai Canal leads from Diamond Head and curves into the ocean at the Ala Wai Yacht Harbor and Magic Island.

$\mathcal{E}$mpress of Britain

Photo by Ray Jerome Baker
Baker-Van Dyke Collection

> The Empress of Britain, accompanied by several tugboats, enters Honolulu Harbor in 1933. Contrasting sharply with the steamship is the four-masted brig at left.

Old Manoa Valley

Λ Ray Jerome Baker stood atop Rocky Hill on the campus of Punahou School to shoot this photograph of Manoa Valley in 1908. The University of Hawaii has been established the year before in the valley. Round Top is the bald hill at left. The large two-story house at middle, right, is the former Frank C. Atherton residence, now the home of the president of the University of Hawaii.

Photo by Ray Jerome Baker
Baker-Van Dyke Collection

*K*amehameha Statue

∨ *The lei-draped statue of King Kamehameha I is surrounded by members of the Hawaii National Guard during Kamehameha Day, June 11. Eight-feet tall and mounted on a high pedestal, the statue stands in front of Ali'iolani Hale, the Judiciary Building in Palace Square. The statue was unveiled by Hawaii's last king, Kalakaua, on February 14, 1883, two days after his coronation across King Street at Iolani Palace.*

*L*ahaina Sunset

⋀ Sunset arrives at Lahaina Harbor. During the mid-19th century, this colorful Maui town became a favorite port-of-call for Pacific whalers. New England and British ships began pouring into the Pacific in 1820 as the news spread about the rich sperm whale grounds off the coast of Japan. The whaling ships did not come to Lahaina to hunt whales but to secure provisions and to give their crews rest and recreation. During the peak year of 1846 a total of 429 ships visited Lahaina. Although the whaleships have long since sailed away, Lahaina is now a thriving tourist center that tries to preserve the salty spirit of the 1880s.

*A*bove Lahaina

∧ In this unusual aerial view of Lahaina the West Maui Mountains, which rise to almost 5,000 feet, provide a dramatic backdrop to this historic seaside community. The mountains block the strong northeast trade winds which blow throughout the Hawaiian Islands and create a natural barrier for the calm open channel between Lahaina and the island of Lanai. In between the mountains and the town the rolling hills are terraced with sugar cane. Lahaina's small boat harbor has a man-made seawall that further protects the many private yachts and charter boats which choose to anchor here today.

Lahaina Harbor

< By the late 1800s the whaling era had ended and Hawaii's commercial center has shifted from Lahaina back to Honolulu. The Pioneer Inn (center with red roof) was built in 1901. It originally had 14 rooms costing $2.50 a night. Travelers who could get by without a warm bath were charged only $1. At the left is the 93-foot Carthaginian II, originally a German schooner but now rebuilt to resemble the type of whaleships that once anchored at Lahaina. An exhibit depicting Hawaii's whaling days has been set up aboard the ship.

Kaanapali Beach Resort

∧ This view of the Kaanapali Beach Resort focuses on the resort's nearly three miles of white sand beach. The three wings of the Hyatt Regency Maui can be seen in the center. The Maui Marriott is the first hotel to the left while the road at right leads to Lahaina. Future plans for the resort, which is now only half-finished, include a Hawaiian Sea Village. This "living museum" will be an authentic recreation of the kinds of coastal villages that existed in Hawaii at the time of Captain Cook's discovery of the Island in 1778.

*K*aanapali Beach Resort

∨ *The Hawaiian phrase* Ka' Ana Pali *can be translated as "the rolling cliffs." It refers to the spacious open ridges behind the coastline which sweep gently to the summit of* Pu'u Kukui, *the highest peak of the West Maui Mountains. Amfac, Inc., a Hawaii company founded in 1849, started to develop the Kaanapali Beach Resort in 1958. This aerial panorama shows (from left to right) the Royal Lahaina in the far distance at left,* the Sheraton-Maui strikingly facing the sea at Black Rock, the low-rise Kaanapali Beach Hotel at center, the twin-towered Whaler condominium, the Whalers Village shopping complex, the Maui Surf, the Kaanapali Alii, and the Maui Marriott. The beach curves around the Marriott to the Hyatt Regency Maui. Behind the Whaler condominium towers is the championship Royal Kaanapali Golf Course.

Leeward Maui

/\ The arid leeward side of Maui gets less rainfall than any other section of Maui coastline. In the center of the photograph is the Polo Beach Club, an eight story condominium in Makena run as a hotel. To the left in the distance is Wailea, a totally planned resort community developed by Alexander & Baldwin. Wailea has two first-class hotels, the large Inter-Continental Maui and the smaller Stouffer Wailea. The island off to the right is uninhabited Kahoolawe.

*S*even Pools

∨ *Off the road between Hana and Kipahulu on East Maui are the "Seven Pools," a popular swimming spot for both tourists and residents alike. The pools are fed by two streams which meet in Kipahulu Valley and flow down to the ocean. In 1969 the valley and pools were made a part of Haleakala National Park. The natural environment of the Kipahulu area was a favorite retreat of pioneer aviator and conservationist Charles Lindbergh. He and his wife, writer Anne Morrow Lingbergh, had a cliffside house here. After his death in 1974 the body of the 72-year old Lindbergh was placed in a wooden coffin and buried in a simple grave next to the Ho'omau Congregational Church which was built in 1857.*

*S*cience City

∧ Haleakala, the large volcano of East Maui, rises 12,000 feet above sea level. Weather near the summit tends to be dry and warm during the summer and cold and damp during the winter. Clouds are heaviest at mid-day. Indirect contrast to the serenity and simple beauty of the mountain is Science City, a secretive complex of government buildings built on the crater's rim. Scientists here are involved in satellite tracking—both ours and theirs—and other space-age experiments.

Haleakala Crater

< *A sightseeing helicopter flies over Haleakala Crater. Today the summit landscape is a fragile cone-pocked reminder of a once-active volcano. Streaks of red, brown, gray and black cinders were left behind by eruptions and lava flows. Hiking is permitted in the crater and there are three cabins maintained by the National Park Service for visitor use. There are also two primitive campgrouds.*

Old Hilo Bay

< This photograph of Byron Bay (Hilo Bay) at Hilo was taken on the Big Island by Ray Jerome Baker in 1908. He aimed his camera back across Byron Bay towards Hilo from a spot near the present Naniloa Surf Hotel and Coconut Island. Several masted ships can be seen at left. At this time Hilo was an important port for the shipping of sugar and other agricultural products to the mainland. The white building at center was used by fishermen.

Liliuokalani Gardens

∨ Liliuokalani Gardens, 30 acres of manicured grounds in Hilo, features an attractive arrangement of pagodas, curved bridges, and stone lanterns in the Edo style. Footpaths meander around the ponds and the plants are representative of both Hawaii and Japan. Hilo is one of the wettest cities in the country and this climate is ideal for gardens and flower growing. Commercially grown orchids and anthuriums are a major source of the city's income.

Kealakekua Bay

∨ A small catamaran drops off snorkelers to explore the underwater world of Kealakekua Bay near Kailua on the Kona Coast of the Big Island. To the left is the white concrete obelisk erected in 1877 (to replace and earlier one) as a monument to Captain James Cook. The first European known to have reached the Hawaiian Islands, Cook stepped ashore at Kealakekua Bay in January 1779 and accepted the hospitality of the island's high chief. Cook sailed away from the bay and then was forced to return when one of his two ships was damaged in a storm. On February 14, 1779 an argument on shore unexpectedly turned into a bloody skirmish. Cook was hit by a club and then stabbed by the Hawaiians with several daggers. He fell at the water's edge and a plaque, submerged during high tide, marks the spot near where he died.

Kilauea Volcano

$\wedge$ Kilauea, in the Big Island's Hawaii Volcanoes National Park, is among the most active volcanoes in the world. Most of its outbursts are relatively mild and the material released is usually slowly moving lava. These flows, however, have destroyed forestland, agricultural crops and even houses in recent years. In 1984, for the first time since 1868, there was a simultaneous eruption of the Kilauea and Mauna Loa volanoes. The residents of Hilo were put on alert but the lava flows never posed a significant danger to the city.

$\mathcal{N}$a Pali Coast

∧ The north shore of Kauai is one of the most beautiful stretches of seashore in the islands. The road past Hanalei ends at Haena and from there a 11-mile hiking trail along the Na Pali Coast leads left to Kalalau Valley. This photograph was taken from the first trail lookout beyond Haena Point.

82

82

*E*merald Mountains

∧ *Kauai's lushly blanketed mountains make it clear why Kauai is nicknamed "The Garden Island." The wettest spot in the world, Mt. Waialeale, is the mist-covered mountain to the right. It averages over 38 feet of rain per year.*

$\mathcal{W}$*aimea* Canyon

∧ *Waimea Canyon on Kauai earned its description of the "Grand Canyon of the Pacific" long ago. It is significantly smaller but to most island visitors the size doesn't matter. The best time to view the canyon is just before sunset when the sun's last rays slide across the cliffs and illuminate the natural rainbow colors of the rocks. Further up the road from Waimea Canyon is Kokee State park where rental cabins are available. An extensive network of trails near the canyon offer more intimate views of this wilderness paradise.*

$\mathcal{H}$analei Bay

∧ Hanalei Bay is a favorite of small-boat sailors who regularly anchor here for weeks at a time. Part of the movie "South Pacific," starring Rossano Brazzi and Mitzi Gaynor, was filmed at Lumahai Beach near here and the 1958 movie's famous mountain, Bali Hai, can be seen across the bay. At the very end of the road heading right is Haena Beach and the beginning of the hiking trail into the spectacular Kalalau Valley. To the near left are townhouses belonging to the Princeville Resort, a 1,000 area recreational development that's divided into a number of separate housing areas.

Acknowledgments

I have found that a book, as most endeavors, requires the time, talents and efforts of many people.

Bennett Hymer very patiently listened to all my ideas, and then finally reduced them to a reasonable and practical publishing package.

Ronn Ronck first absorbed large amounts of information for this book, then wrote the introductory essay and the photo captions. His writing clearly and accurately informs the reader of the facts.

Bill Fong, Leo Gonzalez, and Gregg Ichiki faced the task of viewing large numbers of panoramas, then selecting and arranging the best of them so that the photography is meaningful, exciting and beautiful.

Robert E. Van Dyke and his mother, Gladys R. Van Dyke, curators of the Baker-Van Dyke Collection, provided historical information and photographs by the late Ray Jerome Baker and others to add a dramatic complementary element to the book.

Taking the photographs for PANORAMA HAWAII required the permission, approval, and assistance of many people, mainly boat captains and helicopter pilots.

I wish to express my thanks and appreciation to Linda Kamps, whose efforts were greatly instrumental throughout the project. She was involved in initiating the project, and countless hours were spent in scouting sites, arranging permission to get to where you just can't get, arranging for travel, food, and lodging, directing pilots while I operated the camera, and using her artistic talents in many ways to assure the success of this book.

Many thanks to all.
Jack Rankin

How to Order Photographs

Actual photographic prints of the color panoramas in this book are available. Each print is made directly from the original film, and may be ordered framed, or picture only.

Because of printing and size restriction, some of the panoramas have been cropped to smaller than their full size for use in the book. Photographic prints ordered will show the full scene.

Prints may be ordered in contact print size (negative size), and also enlargements that are two, four, or eight times the negative size. Most prints in the book are contact size.

In addition to the color panoramas in this book, the complete portfolio consists of approximately two hundred scenes of the four major islands.

For information on sizes and prices, please contact Panorama Photography Inc., P.O. Box 9262, Ontario, California 91762. Phone 714-986-5305. In Hawaii call 808-254-1896.

Other Mutual Titles

Celebration: A Portrait of Hawaii
A deluxe coffee table book. Songs,
photographs, illustrations and an informative
narrative present a fascinating image of
Hawaii, including its music, culture, dance,
history, and legends. Winner of two
New York Art Director Club Awards
for design and cover. $29.95

Hawaiian Journey
A pictorial history of Hawaii from the
arrival of Captain Cook to the present day.
Over 200 duotone photographs. Now into its
seventh printing.
128 pps. soft cover $8.95 ISBN 0-935180-04-4

*Hawaiian Yesterdays: Historical photographs
by Ray Jerome Baker*
Now into its fifth printing. Old Hawaii
as it really was. People, places, and events.
256 pps., 600 color-tinted and duotone
nostalgic photographs.
$19.95 softcover

*History Makers of Hawaii:
A Biographical Dictionary by A. Grove Day*
Over 500 movers and shakers of Hawaii's
exotic history, 100 legendary figures and
thousands of other facts for easy reference.
192 pps., $16.95 casebound

Stories of Hawaii by Jack London
Thirteen yarns drawn from the famous
author's love affair with Hawaii Nei. $2.95

A Hawaiian Reader
Thirty-seven selections from the literature
of the past hundred years including such
writers as Mark Twain, Robert Louis
Stevenson and James Jones. $2.95

Best South Seas Stories
Fifteen writers capture all the romance
and exotic adventure of the legendary South
Pacific including James A. Michener, James
Norman Hall, W. Somerset Maugham, and
Herman Melville. $2.95

The Spell of Hawaii
A companion volume to *A Hawaiian Reader*.
Twenty-four selections from the exotic
literary heritage of the islands. $2.95

How to Order More
Panorama Hawaii
and other Mutual titles
Send check or money order to
Mutual Publishing
2055 No. King Street, Suite 202
Honolulu, Hawaii 96819
All prices include book rate mailing U.S.A.
(Allow 3 to 4 weeks)
Add an additional 20 percent for air mail
delivery
For further information and trade inquiries
telephone (808) 845-9954